Drew
is just like
YOU!

Cover and book design by Lucia Benito

978-1-7335462-6-3

Printed in the United States of America
Published by KiCam Projects
www.KiCamProjects.com

For anyone
who might look different:

At times you might feel
like you just don't fit,
but believe in yourself
-don't ever quit!

Hi! I'm an active little girl,
and my name is Drew.
You're just like me
and I'm just like you!

My arm might look different-
yes, it's true.
But I can still do the things
that other kids do.

I like to ride my bike;
my daddy taught me how.
It took a few tries,
but I'm great at it now.

I play soccer;
I love playing with my friends.
I play hard
from the start of the game
right to the end.

My mommy and I
like to exercise;
we do lots of things together.
We'll even build a snowman
in the cold winter weather.

During the summer
we go swimming,
one of my favorite
things to do.
I love being in the water.
How about you?

I even have a pig
that I take
to the county fair.
Lots of kids do it;
it's really fun when I'm there.

I don't have any limits;
I'm a fun-loving girl.
No matter what it is,
I'll give it a whirl.
I run, jump, and play;
I do it every day!
I'm good at a lot of things;
I don't let one little difference
get in the way.

When something
looks different,
or not quite the same,
there's no reason
to feel sorry;
there's no one to blame.

In case you've forgotten,
my name is Drew.
I'd love to have some fun
and play with YOU!

My Family

Our family would like to thank everyone who has encouraged Drew to be herself and find her way in the world. Your endless love and support have been amazing.

We especially thank Molly and The Lucky Fin Project. You have created a great community for kids and families living with a limb difference. The education and inspiration have been our saving grace!

And we also wish to thank Lori, Jennifer, and the team at KiCam for providing us with a platform to raise awareness, educate, and celebrate differences.